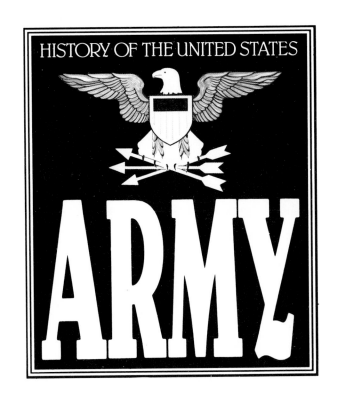

HISTORY OF THE UNITED STATES

ARMY

HISTORY OF THE UNITED STATES

ARMY

First published by
Chevprime Limited
27 Swinton Street,
London WC1

Printed in Italy

ISBN 1-85361-064-X

Victorious American troops
from the 28th Infantry
Division join in the Victory
Parade down the Champs
Elysées on 25 August 1944,
four days after the liberation
of Paris.

had so far played little part in the anti-French fighting was sent under the command of Colonel George Washington to attack the French at Fort Duquesne, constructed on the confluence of the Allegheny and Monongahela Rivers, thereby freeing Pennsylvania of foreign influence. Overwhelmed by superior numbers and forced to surrender, the Virginians were released and sent back home.

During the fourth and final stage of the lengthy Franco-British conflict, the Seven Years War (1756-63), Britain sent strong naval forces and 25,000 regular troops to fight alongside the American colonial regiments placed in regular service and the volunteer militia units. After an initial setback in which a combined force of 16,000 regulars and militia failed to take Fort Ticonderoga, victory followed upon victory until French influence in the Americas was all but destroyed.

In 1758 Louisburg was captured by regular forces after a text-book siege and Fort Frontenac fell in more irregular fashion to a force of 3,000 militia. Quebec fell to British regulars in 1759, a victory made Pyrrhic by the death of their commander Major General James Wolfe in the battle, whilst the river forts of Niagara and Ticonderoga surrendered to a mixed regular-militia force under the command of General Amherst.

When seventy years of intermittent fighting was finally brought to a close by the Treaty of Paris in 1763, Britain and her colonies were left in total mastery of the American continent.

However problems soon arose from this very fact. The colonial volunteer-militia which had borne the brunt of the fighting in the first three wars and had made sizeable contributions in the fourth, had developed their own style of fighting far more suited to the wilderness than that adopted by the more conventional British regulars. They had learned to fight away from home in wars which did not directly affect their own or their families' well-being. They had in fact become in every respect an army which no longer felt it necessary to rely on the British for help or protection.

Both Britain and France had Indian allies in their conflicts, and eventually learned that the rigid formations of European warfare were unsuited to American conditions. On 9 July 1755, the British commander-in-chief in America, Edward Braddock, was ambushed and defeated at the battle of the Monongahela near Fort Duquesne by a smaller mixed force of French and Indians. He and half his force were killed, but George Washington who was a volunteer with the expedition, helped lead the remainder back to Virginia.

2: THE AMERICAN REVOLUTION

With the Treaty of Paris of 1763 and the end of the French Wars, both Britain and her colonists looked forward to a period of stability but, as so often happens, peace brought with it new-found tensions. Nearly bankrupted by the War, Britain found herself having to station 10,000 extra troops in the colonies which were now expanding fast to fill the void left by the French.

New taxes would have to be raised as a matter of priority and it was to her colonies, whom she felt had gained most directly from the victory, that Britain turned. Steps were taken to increase taxation on imports and exports through the Navigation Acts, existing legislation was enforced more rigorously and plans were made to bring the increasingly independence-minded colonists more firmly under direct governmental control.

The colonists on the other hand resented the presence of the redcoats whom they saw more as a restraint on territorial growth than a protection against the frontier Indians whom they had earlier proved inept in fighting. More fundamentally they were adamant that in providing excellent militia throughout the Wars, the costs of which had been borne locally, they had contributed more than adequately to the campaign and should not now have to suffer higher taxation.

Initial half-hearted Parliamentary attempts to raise taxation through the Sugar and Stamp Acts were abandoned in the face of peaceful resistance and local boycotts. Britain realized that if she were to stem the rising tide of independence sweeping the colonies she would have to act with a newly-found sense of firmness and resolution. Her fateful opportunity came when in 1773, in response to the recently passed Tea Act, a group of Bostonians thinly disguised as Indians boarded ships in the harbor, broke into the holds and unceremoniously dumped their valuable cargoes of tea overboard. Parliament over-reacted unwisely and in haste. Punitive legislation, known locally as the "Intolerable Acts," was passed, closing the port of Boston and placing Massachusetts under military rule. The stage was set for armed resistance.

LEXINGTON GREEN

Determined to resist military rule, the Massachusetts Provincial Congress at once prepared for action by stockpiling ammunition and supplies in Concord, a small settlement some 20 miles from Boston. General Gage, the commander of the British garrison, upon learning of this

The British victory at Quebec on 13 September 1759 broke French resistance in Canada, but was marred by the death of General James Wolfe who was one of the finest military leaders of the eighteenth century. This famous painting is by the Pennsylvanian-born artist Benjamin West (1738-1820).

from his network of spies, immediately sent a force of 700 men to seize the illegal stores. However, the minutemen, an elite among the militia, were forewarned of the coming military and formed on the village green at Lexington to block their advance. A short sharp battle ensued on the morning of 19 April after which the militia retired having sustained 8 dead. The redcoats proceeded to Concord where they destroyed the remaining stores before beginning the long return march to Boston. Their route was harried throughout by militiamen sniping at them from vantage points along the way to the extent that they were only saved by a relief force sent from Boston.

By the end of the day the British regulars had sustained nearly 275 casualties and the militiamen 95, a demonstration of the latter's excellent use of guerrilla tactics.

The fuze of insurrection was now lit. Within days the British garrison was under siege from the New England militia, and forces from Connecticut under Benedict Arnold and from Vermont under Ethan Allen had seized the key forts of Ticonderoga and Crown Point.

After a short period of stalemate during which both sides steadily received reinforcements, the British began to fortify Dorchester Heights to the south of Boston, and the colonists Bunker Hill at the neck of the Charleston peninsula to the north. Inexplicably the work party sent to Bunker Hill began to fortify Breed's Hill instead, thus presenting the British with an irresistible target. On the afternoon of 17 June 1775 General Howe was dispatched with 2,200 men to dislodge the militiamen then occupying Breed's Hill in fairly equal numbers. Although they succeeded in their third attempt the British sustained over 1,000 killed and injured in what became known erroneously as the Battle of Bunker Hill. The colonists became convinced, however overoptimistically under the circumstances, that their irregulars were more than a match for the British redcoats.

THE BIRTH OF AN ARMY

Britain determined to fight the War by the implementation of the tried and tested tactics of large-scale set-piece battlefield engagements supported by a naval blockade. However, this necessitated a period of intransigence during which the garrison was steadily increased for the anticipated conflict ahead.

Foreseeing the need for a regular, disciplined force to protect the colonies against the inevitable onslaught, the Second Continental Congress adopted the irregular New England Army assembled around Boston as the Continental Army on 14 June 1775, and the next day appointed George Washington of Virginia as its Commander-in-Chief. The American Army had been born.

Although Washington was appointed primarily for political reasons in an attempt to unite the southern colonies behind a conflict which many still saw as a northern irrelevancy, the choice proved to be fortuitous. Washington was an inspired and dedicated leader who despite his limited battlefield experience in the Indian and French Wars nevertheless enjoyed a tremendous degree of military perception and foresight.

Steps were taken immediately to form an army of 20,000 men under the command of four major-generals and eight brigadiers, all of whom had seen service in New England or in the British Army itself.

Initially the British swept aside the Minutemen in their advance to Concord. Subsequently, however, they were to lose a quarter of their force. This cartoon was engraved by the American patriot Paul Revere (1735-1810).

Early enlistment was disappointing as many colonists were unwilling to sacrifice even a year away from their farms and families.

Despite the perilous lack of supplies (he was relying heavily upon booty taken from a few captured supply ships to provision his forces), Washington decided to launch a major expedition into the north in the hopes of adding Canada to the coalition of rebellious states whilst securing a potential invasion route from the St. Lawrence through Lake Champlain to the vital Hudson Valley.

The expedition consisting of 2,000 men under the command of Major General Schuyler of New York met with limited success. Montreal fell on 13 November but Quebec held firm. Decimated by illness and desertions, the American forces made a last disastrous attempt to storm the city under the cover of a snowstorm on the night of 13 November 1775. Brigadier Montgomery was killed, Colonel Arnold wounded and the attackers thrown into disarray. When the British received reinforcements and counter-attacked in June 1776 the colonists retreated without a fight, leaving Canada and the St. Lawrence firmly in British hands.

This defeat was mitigated in part by the British withdrawal from Boston on 17 March 1776. Although General Howe, who had succeeded General Gage, made the decision to abandon Boston on sound military grounds, the militia had placed artillery on the recently captured Dorchester Heights and Nook's Hill to harrass the garrison. Although Halifax, to which the British redeployed, was strategically far safer, the colonists saw the evacuation as their first concrete victory.

THE DECLARATION OF INDEPENDENCE

On 4 July 1776 the Declaration of Independence was proclaimed and a struggle for home rule became at once a war for total independence. However, the colonists were far from united and many were actively against the continuation of hostilities. Supplies for the Continental Army were kept to a minimum, enlistments remained short term and the incidence of desertions high. Although in theory the Continental Army consisted of 110 battalions or 80,000 men, in reality it rarely numbered more than 30,000 of whom no

Washington led his men across the River Delaware in a fierce snowstorm on Christmas night, 1776 and defeated the Hessians at Trenton.

Left: The Continental Congress drew up the Declaration of Independence in Philadelphia in 1776 by which time the war was already a year old.

Overleaf: The Battle of Valcour Island, Lake Champlain took place on 28 October 1776. The makeshift American fleet under the command of Benedict Arnold was defeated by a stronger British force. Most of the American ships were captured or sunk, but the battle had delayed the British advance on Fort Ticonderoga and instead caused them to withdraw to winter quarters in Canada.

Some Continental Army Uniforms from the early years of the war. The man in the foreground is one of 'Morgan's Rifles' (see page 27).

following year.

The infantry carried a hotch-potch of weapons varying from the British "Brown Bess" 0.753 caliber musket to the Pennsylvania long rifle, so lethal in the hands of a marksman. As the War progressed, an increasing number of French 0.69 caliber Charleville muskets reached the American forces but, even so, weapons were never standardized.

Generally speaking, the artillery fared no better, although by the end of the War domestic armories were producing standard 4-, 12- and 18-pounder cannon along standard French lines to supplement the ordnance captured earlier from the British.

Despite early attempts at centralized dress-regulations, uniforms remained a sea of divergent color throughout the War. Many units refused to adopt the brown coats recommended by Congress in 1775 and those that did found that the dyes supplied were so unreliable that "regulation" coats varied in hue from light sand to dark umber.

Although the standard infantry blue coat of 1779 with its distinctive lapel facings (white for New England, buff for New York and New Jersey, red for Pennsylvania, Delaware, Maryland and Virginia, and blue with white for the southern states) proved more popular, by the time of its introduction many states simply had neither the finances nor the resources to introduce it.

Despite the introduction of nearly 30,000 uniforms supplied by France between 1776 and 1778, the Continental Army finished the War as it began it, dressed in a mixture of uniforms and colors cobbled together by any means possible. Prior to 1778, military training was piecemeal and often ineffectual. Veterans of the militia who had relied traditionally on enthusiasm and woodsmanship rather than iron discipline for success, now felt unwilling to adopt what many saw as discredited British regular tactics, and as a consequence were of little value in open battle.

Matters improved considerably in 1778 when Washington appointed Frederick Wilhelm, Baron von Steuben, a former staff officer in the Prussian Army of Frederick the Great, to be his Inspector-General.

Von Steuben at once set up at Valley Forge a training program which was highly professional, comprehensive and adapted specifically for American conditions. Cadres taught personally by Von Steuben returned to their units to inaugurate local training programs, thus ensuring that the new tactics were disseminated throughout the Army with the minimum of delay. In 1779, at the Baron's instigation, the

more than half were battle-ready at any one time. Consequently Washington was forced to supplement his forces with locally raised militia whose standards varied greatly and who remained solidly under the influence of the domestic legislatures, with the result that rarely, if ever, did he enjoy the military independence for which he yearned.

THE CONTINENTAL ARMY

At the outset, the Continental Army consisted almost entirely of infantry supplemented by cavalry and artillery supplied by the militia. This was far from satisfactory and in the summer of 1776 Colonel Henry Knox was tasked with the formation of four battalions of artillery each consisting of 10 companies equipped with between 6 to 10 guns per company. A cavalry formation of four regular regiments each of 360 light dragoons organized into six troops was created in the

As an emerging neutral, the United States found herself deeply involved in a war in which she had no obvious interest. Determined to avoid actual combat, Congress negotiated Jay's Treaty of 1794 with Britain under the terms of which the latter withdrew her remaining troops from her outposts in the American west. Seeing this, however erroneously, as a flagrantly pro-British act, France immediately accelerated her seizure of American shipping. Congress countered by authorizing the mobilization, although only for three months, of 80,000 militia and the formation of a Provisional Army for the protection of domestic harbors and borders. The anticipated invasion never came, the French threat abated, and in 1800 Congress felt secure enough to disband the Army.

President Thomas Jefferson took the bold step in 1803 of purchasing the State of Louisiana, including the vital port of St Louis, from an impecunious France for only $15 million, thus securing once and for all a secure trade route to the south.

WAR WITH BRITAIN

When Thomas Jefferson assumed the Presidency in 1801 he brought with him an avowed policy of prosperity through peace. The army was reduced to 3,000 men and the navy virtually scrapped.

The resumption of hostilities between Britain and France however led to an intolerable increase in the harrassment of American merchant shipping, exacerbated by the new British policy of pressing American seamen into service in the Royal Navy. Early American attempts at a trade embargo failed, causing far more suffering to the domestic producers than the European merchants. Demands for war against Britain, particularly from southern and western traders most hit by the British blockade, grew to fever-pitch until Congress was forced by the pressure of public opinion to declare war on Great Britain on 18 June 1812.

On the face of it Britain was vastly superior in manpower and resources. Her regular army numbered 300,000 supported by a large militia, her fleet of 700 ships included 125 ships of the line and her treasury was full. To counter this the United States had an army of only 11,000 including 5,000 raw recruits, a militia not contracted to serve abroad and, to fight a war in which control of the seas would be crucial, a fleet of less than 20 ships including no more than six frigates.

Britain, however, was currently fighting Napoleon in Europe and could only afford to regard this latest confrontation as a minor irritant to be contained until Napoleon was crushed, after which forces for its prosecution

would become available. She could not afford to reinforce the Canadian garrison of 6,000 regulars and 2,000 militia for long, nor could she hope to release more than the 80 ships then engaged on blockade duty.

The United States Army itself was suffering from years of neglect. Supplies were short, training and morale were low, and experienced officers rare. With the exception of the Corps of Engineers, who had established a small academy at West Point (later to become the United States Military Academy), in 1802 support units were sadly ill-equipped to wage an all-out war.

The United States Army could at least now

William Henry Harrison (1773-1841) became a national hero after the Battle of Tippecanoe Creek. His reputation for ruthlessness in battle stood him in good stead when he ran for the Presidency. He died of pneumonia just one month after his inauguration as President.

British infantry advance during the Battle of Lundy's Lane, Ontario (25 July 1814). This was the bloodiest battle of the war, but was also indecisive.

boast a plentiful supply of domestically produced weapons, notably the 0.69 caliber flintlock musket and the 0.59 caliber flintlock cavalry pistol manufactured at the government arsenals at Springfield and Harper's Ferry respectively, and uniforms had now taken on a degree of regimentation.

United States Army soldiers now at least looked like soldiers; whether or not they would act as such when faced by a well-trained and disciplined enemy remained to be seen.

The war began badly for the American land forces when three independent offensives against Canada were repulsed with heavy losses.

By the end of 1812, Fort Dearborn (now Chicago) had been destroyed by pro-British Indians and its inhabitants massacred; Fort Mackinac and Detroit had fallen to a small British force commanded by General Brock, placing the entire Northwest territory under British control; a force of 900 militia under the inexperienced Major General van Rensselaer had been forced to surrender; and an attack on Montreal had ended in a costly fiasco.

The next year was only a little better for the Americans. An early attempt by Brigadier Henry Harrison, the hero of Tippecanoe, to recapture Detroit ended in failure made even more

The death of General
Zebulon M. Pike, after whom
Pike's Peak is named. He was
killed in the successful taking
of York (now Toronto),
Canada on 24 April 1813.

Similar attempts to bring lower Canada under American influence in late 1813 ended in unmitigated disaster when forces totalling 10,000 men led by General Wilkinson and Brigadier Hampton fell back in disorder when confronted by vastly inferior British forces.

One of the bloodiest engagements of the year was fought in the south between Andrew Jackson, an avowed Indian hater, and the Creek Indians. In the summer of 1813 the Creeks attacked Fort Mims, in the southern Mississippi Territory, massacring over 500 men, women and children. In retaliation, Jackson, with a band of 600 regulars, 2,000 militia and hundreds of friendly Indians, pursued the 900 Creeks to Horseshoe Bend, destroyed them in battle and thereafter set about a systematic massacre of the survivors every bit as bloody as that perpetrated at the Fort.

Throughout 1813 the Royal Navy continued its blockade of American ports, denying the tiny American Navy access to the seas.

American attempts to seize lower Canada in 1814 met with failure. The British were now being reinforced by veterans of the Napoleonic Wars and decided to take the initiative. In August a force under the command of Major General Ross captured Washington, burning the Capitol and White House before withdrawing in good order. Subsequent attempts to take Baltimore were less successful in the face of a spirited defense engineered by Samuel Smith and his force of 10,000 Maryland militiamen.

The last great battle of the War, the disastrous British attack on New Orleans in which over 2,000 regulars were killed or injured, took place on 8 January 1815, some two weeks after peace had been negotiated.

For the second time in America's short history, her regular forces and militia had come together to defend the nation. It was becoming increasingly apparent, however, that despite the militia's occasional bravery (they had comprised the majority of troops at New Orleans and in the defense of Baltimore), America's future security would inevitably depend almost exclusively on the proficiency of the regular armed forces.

unpalatable by the subsequent massacre of 500 prisoners by their Indian captors. A small force under General Pike successfully stormed York (now Toronto), a victory lessened when Pike himself was killed in an accidental powder magazine explosion. An amphibious assault under the command of Colonel Winfield Scott and Commander Oliver Hazard Perry of the navy took Forts George and Queenston on the western shore of the Niagara River.

Subsequently, Commander Perry secured Lake Erie, destroying a six-ship Royal Navy flotilla in the process, enabling American forces to continue unimpeded into upper Canada.

4: THE INDIAN AND MEXICAN WARS

Popular support for the Armed Forces soon diminished with the coming of peace and cutbacks inevitably followed to the extent that by 1823 there were no more than 6,000 men serving the colors.

A number of major changes were, however, taking place within the Army. The Military Academy at West Point, which had been pioneered by the Corps of Engineers, was expanded in 1816 and the cadets given ceremonial gray uniforms reminiscent of those worn by their forebears at Chippewa and Lundy's Lane.

Brevet Major Sylvanus Thayer, appointed superintendent in the following year, immediately set about a number of administrative and educational reforms within the Academy, expanding its curriculum to incorporate infantry, artillery and cavalry tactics. During the 30 years that followed, over 1,000 cadets graduated from the Academy, of whom nearly one half remained as career officers to give the US Army its first real professional continuity.

Under the auspices of Secretary for War John Calhoun, an artillery school was established at Fortress Monroe at the mouth of Chesapeake Bay and an infantry school at Jefferson Barracks, St Louis, in which whole units rather than individuals attended training courses of up to a year's duration.

Although the United States met with no foreign enemies during this period, the Indian problem remained to the extent that the Army found itself involved in three wars before the lands east of the Mississippi were finally pacified.

During the First Seminole War of 1817, Andrew Jackson, the inveterate Indian fighter and now commander of the Southern Department, led 800 regulars and 1,000 Georgian militia, (later supplemented by 1,000 Tennesseans), into Spanish Florida in pursuit of bands of Seminole and Creek Indians recently incited by rogue British adventurers to raid across the border. Hanging two British traders for allegedly aiding the Indians, Jackson soon gained total control of central and western Florida. When Spain issued half-hearted political protests, a solution was speedily reached and the entire area ceded to the United States in exchange for a small cash sum.

The second of the Indian Wars, or Black Hawk

American soldiers capture Monterrey, Mexico on 24 September 1846 while under the command of General Zachary Taylor (1784-1850).

War, took place on the Illinois and Wisconsin frontiers in 1832, after Chief Black Hawk recrossed the Mississippi with 500 warriors and 1,000 women and children to reclaim his lost ancestral lands. Alarmed by this unilateral act of aggression, the Illinois government dispatched 1,000 militia supported by 500 regulars under the command of Colonel Henry Atkinson to the troubled area. Realising that his position was hopeless, Black Hawk attempted to escape north into Wisconsin Territory before recrossing the river but was brought to battle first at Wisconsin Heights and subsequently on the Bad Axe River where his forces were annihilated.

The final and largest Indian War, the Second Seminole War, began in 1835. Essentially a guerrilla campaign, the Seminole chief Osceola shunned from meeting the US Army in open combat, preferring to harry small detachments and lightly defended outposts from the relative safety of his strongholds in the swamps. The campaign which was marked by savagery on both sides was only brought to a successful conclusion when Osceola and several of his chiefs were tricked into attending a peace conference under a flag of truce and subsequently arrested.

Sac and Fox Indians were forcibly resettled in Western Iowa after being decisively beaten at the Battle of the Bad Axe River, Wisconsin on 2 August 1832.

Confederate soldiers fire a
piece of heavy artillery.

A 15 inch Rodney Siege gun.

Ulysses Simpson Grant (1822-85) was the 'fighting general' Lincoln had been seeking, but his victories were won at the cost of many lives.

The Union was badly defeated at the Battle of Bull Run, 21st July 1864. It was the first major battle of the Civil War.

EARLY CONFLICT

The War commenced with a peroid of inactivity during which both protagonists concentrated on the training of their raw recruits. However, in June 1861, pressured by public opinion, Lincoln ordered Brigadier McDowell, then stationed south of Washington with 30,000 men, to advance into Virginia.

General Beauregard, in command of 22,000 Confederates at Manassas Junction a few miles to the south, moved his forces behind Bull Run to await McDowell's slowly advancing Federals.

The two virtually equal armies met on the morning of 21 July, at which time each immediately attempted to turn the other's right flank. Although initially successful, McDowell's forces were halted by an unexpected counter-attack and turned. Defeat disintegrated into a rout until, unable to regain control, McDowell was forced to order a withdrawal to the outskirts of Washington.

For the rest of the year both armies faced each other uneasily, neither wishing to make a move until its numbers and strength had been increased.

THE WESTERN CAMPAIGN

The western campaign of 1862 began well for the Union, whose forces in that area outnumbered the Confederates by nearly five to one. Fort Henry on the Tennessee River fell to Grant on 6 February, followed by Fort Donelson some twelve miles to the east on the Cumberland River a week later. By early March over 15,000 Confederate prisoners had fallen into Union hands and the road south into Tennessee lay wide open and undefended.

Halleck, in overall command of the Western Theatre, ordered Grant to proceed to Shiloh to await the arrival of Buell's Ohio Army before proceeding deeper into enemy territory. Fully apprised of the Union plans, General Johnston, in command of the local defenders, elected to attack Grant at Shiloh before Buell could join him.

After a hard march Johnston fell upon Grant on the morning of 6 April, taking the latter completely by surprise. However at his very moment of victory Johnston was wounded, command passed to Beauregard and the Confederate attack was halted. During the course of the following night Grant received 17,000 reinforcements from Buell and in the morning was able to regain the initiative. During the course of the battle the North sustained 13,000 casualties, over 20 per cent of their entire force, but the South itself had lost 11,000 men from the 40,000 committed and had been forced to retire. The road into Tennessee remained open.

When Memphis fell on 6 June the central Mississippi fell firmly into federal hands. Later that month a force of 18,000 men under General Butler, supported by a flotilla of 46 ships under Captain Farragut, sailed into the lower Mississippi, fought their way past the coastal forts

Robert E. Lee (1807-79) was one of history's great generals. He led the Confederate forces throughout the war.

On 15 February 1862, Grant led the Union forces that captured Fort Donelson on the Cumberland River, Tennessee.

and captured the vital sea port of New Orleans.

By early August, Baton Rouge and Natchez had fallen, leaving the lower river securely under Union control. Lincoln had only to take the small stretch between Port Hudson and Vicksberg to fulfil his aim of bisecting the Confederacy.

Far from down-hearted, the Confederates immediately planned a massive counter-offensive in the West. General Bragg, who had replaced Beauregard after the latter's surrender of Corinth, moved north against Buell in the hopes of inducing neutral Kentucky into the Con-federacy. However despite severe losses inflic-ted on the Union at the battles of Perryville and Stones River in October and December 1862, Buell's forces proved too powerful, Kentucky remained undecided and Bragg was forced to fall back upon Chattanooga.

In the East, 1862 began in stalemate with General McClellan assiduously refusing to move his 150,000 Union troops south against the far smaller numbers of General Johnston, without adequate preparation. Eventually, having re-tained McDowell and his 30,000 men for the pro-tection of Washington, Lincoln grudgingly consented to McClellan moving the residue of his troops by sea to Fort Monroe, to the south-east of Richmond, to put pressure on the enemy capital.

Despite his having more than enough troops to complete the mission, McClellan moved with such caution that the Confederates were able to gather 70,000 troops to meet him. Panic-stricken, McClellan requested and was granted McDowell's 30,000 troops as reinforcements, but this contingency was foreseen by Davis who immediately dispatched Jackson with 17,000 men to threaten Washington.

Although never more than a diversion, Jackson succeeded in drawing off all available troops in the Washington area, including McDowell's much needed reinforcements, before retiring in good order down the Shenandoah Valley.

Simultaneously, Johnston attacked the heart-ily demoralized McClellan on 31 May at Fair Oaks and Seven Pines but could not dent his lines. The badly wounded Johnston was replaced by Robert E. Lee, who immediately mounted a spirited offensive culminating in the Seven Days' Battle (25 June-1 July), after which the Union forces pulled back south-east to the protective mantle of their naval base on the James River.

Lee followed, constantly harrassing the still numerically superior enemy, suffering 11,000 casualties in the process.

McClellan was ordered back to Washington to support General Pope, recently brought from the West to rejuvenate sagging Union spirits. As

Lee's invasion of Maryland was stopped at Sharpsburg (Antietam) in September 1862.

Andrew 'Stonewall' Jackson (1824-63) was an outstanding leader of the Confederate cavalry. His death deprived Lee of his most valuable supporter.

After the Civil War, Congress reduced its expenditure on the army. However, the Krag bolt-action breech-loading rifle was introduced in 1893 and is shown in this illustration of an American infantryman by Frederic Remington.

Right: After the war, the army became increasingly involved in the suppression of industrial unrest - a duty detested by the ordinary soldier.

Below: Troops protect a train during the Pullman railroad strike of 1894.

leadership the post-war Army enjoyed some of the finest training establishments in the world. The Corps of Engineers relinquished control of West Point Military Academy in 1866, after which its curriculum was broadened considerably. Several post-graduate professional schools were set up and the Artillery School at Fort Monroe was reopened in 1868 after a gap of eight years. Most important of all, the School of Application for Infantry and Cavalry, later to become the General Service and Staff College, was opened at Fort Leavenworth.

INTERNAL STRIFE
Morale within the Army hit its lowest ebb during the 1870s and 1880s when troops were called out to curb the increasingly violent spate of strikes then occurring throughout the industrial North-East. Throughout, the Army exercised tremendous restraint, often in the face of extensive provocation, and in only one instance, during the Pullman Strike of 1894, was a rioter killed by military action. Even so the role of the military in domestic matters was questioned, and in several instances individual states and the federal government were deeply divided as to whether or not to employ troops.

As a direct result many governors and local legislatures began to see the reformation of the volunteer militia as the only way of ensuring the preservation of their powers against encroachment from Washington. By 1892 every State had its own local force, or "National Guard" as they began to be known, free of Federal control. By the turn of the century over 100,000 men, mainly middle-class conservatives, had enrolled in the Guard which was by then considerably larger and in many respects more influential than the regular army it was intended to support.

Indian leaders were dealt with mercilessly by post-war governments. This public hanging of the leaders of a Sioux uprising in 1862 was not an especially uncommon occurrence.

Above: The Wagon Box Fight between the Army and Sioux in 1867. The Indian Wars were bloody and uncompromising with quarter neither asked for nor given.

Above right: Sitting Bull (1834?-90) was the most famous of all the Sioux.

Opposite top left: George Armstrong Custer (1839-76).

Opposite top right: *Custer's Last Stand* by Otto Becker.

Opposite center right: Geronimo (1834-1909) with three fellow Apaches photographed after his surrender in 1886.

Opposite bottom right: A mass grave for the dead of Wounded Knee, 1890.

THE INDIAN WARS

West of the Mississippi some 270,000 Indians, over 100,000 of whom were potential combatants, co-habited uneasily with two million white settlers. Up to 9,000 soldiers, many but not all of whom were cavalry, were allotted the thankless task of policing this huge, hostile area. Caught between a humanitarian faction which regarded all Indian deaths as murder and the frontiersmen who wanted the Indian lands at any cost, the role of the Army as mediator was all but impossible.

The Plains Indians themselves constituted arguably the finest light cavalry of their era. Brave and tenacious in the extreme, they were at the same time cruel, suspicious and argumentative.

The Indian Wars, which lasted from 1866 to 1890 and which resulted in the deaths of 2,000 soldiers and 6,000 Indians, invariably relied on the use of converging columns to force the Indians to stand and fight, on the wholesale destruction of their camps, livestock and shelter and on the employment of friendly Indians both as scouts and combatants.

The initial campaign, fought in the South against the Cheyenne, Arapahoes and Kiowas, ended in the year-long Red River War of 1874 when 3,000 soldiers herded the unhappy Indians into reservations in present-day Oklahoma.

The Sioux federation in the North with its 30,000 members proved a more difficult adversary. Enraged by what they considered a flagrant breach of earlier treaties, the Sioux under the leadership of Red Cloud left their reservation, joined the "hunting bands" of Sitting Bull and migrated en masse to their ancestral homes in the Black Hills of Montana.

General Sheridan, commanding a division in

Missouri, was ordered to return the recalcitrant Sioux to their reservations. One column of 1,000 men supported by 250 Crow and Shoshone allies under the command of Brigadier Crook, marched north from Fort Fetterman in Wyoming. A second column of 450 soldiers and 25 Crow under Colonel Gibbon was dispatched against the Sioux encampments in south-east Montana and a third force of 950 soldiers and 40 Indian scouts, including the 7th Cavalry, under the overall command of Brigadier Terry, moved westward from Fort Abraham Lincoln.

Crook's column was attacked by 1,500 Sioux and Cheyenne warriors along the Rosebud Creek just north of the Montana border, and in the ensuing six-hour battle was so badly mauled that it was forced to retire. Unaware of this setback or of the enemy's vastly under-estimated numbers, the remaining columns continued. Custer and the 7th Cavalry were detached to the Little Big-Horn to drive the Sioux into the arms of the waiting infantry. Inexplicably Custer split his already stretched command into three independent columns. Two of the columns under Benteen and Reno were able to reunite before being brought to battle by an overwhelming number of Sioux and managed to hold out for two days before the survivors were relieved by Terry. Custer

battlefield standards.

The Guard, reserves and volunteers were augmented by draftees conscripted under the Selective Service Act of May 1917. Administration of the draft was vested in local citizens boards and originally limited to men between the ages of 18 and 30 although this was later extended to those between 18 and 45. Substitutions and bounties, so shamelessly abused in the Civil War draft, were specifically outlawed.

The initial Act increased the regular Army strength to 286,000, the Guards to 400,000 and allowed for one million volunteers but these numbers were steadily increased as the War progressed until, by the Armistice of November 1918, over 3.6 million men were serving in 62 divisions.

Training and supply remained a nightmare. Still on a peacetime footing, the home market was totally incapable of supplying so large a force without assistance, so much so that it became necessary to supplement Springfield rifles with the arguably better British Lee Enfields and to accept Allied, particularly French, machine-guns and artillery.

INTO ACTION

As Pershing led his small force to France he was ever-mindful of its deficiencies in training and of his orders to retain it as a "separate and distinct component" free of French or British control. Accordingly he refused to commit his men to action without a further period of training in all aspects of trench warfare, demanding instead that they be placed in a quiet sector of the line until able to acclimatize.

Recognizing the degree of exhaustion of all the major Armies, yet failing totally to realize the lack of preparedness of the Americans, the German High Command determined to launch a final major offensive before United States involvement could swing the balance in favor of the Allies.

Without warning, a 3.5 million-man offensive was launched against the British and French positions. The initial attack launched on 21 March 1918 against 50 miles of the British front met initially with limited success but failed in its overall task of breaching the British lines. A second attack one month later, also launched against the British, was supported by a feint against the French in the region of the Chemin des Dames to the north-east of Paris. Unknown to the Germans, that sector had recently been taken over by exhausted troops brought from the north for rest and recuperation. The feint was a total success and within three days the Germans were on the Marne within 50 miles of Paris, their

George S. Patton (1885-1945) who was an unofficial aide to Pershing in 1915.

deepest penetration since August 1914.

Two divisions of American soldiers and Marines were rushed to the aid of the French, taking up defensive positions around Chateau-Thierry. Despite their total lack of battle experience the green "doughboys" played a major part in halting the advance, before themselves going on to the offensive in Belleau Wood.

When Ludendorff's exhausted and dispirited Germans made their final desperate assault in June they were halted by, among others, 10 American divisions. United States troops were by now arriving at the rate of 250,000 per month and were eager to play a full part in the coming push to Berlin.

FORWARD TO VICTORY

The Allied offensive when it came had two basic objectives: the elimination of the three salients encroaching into positions held by the British in the North, the French in the center and the Americans in the South, and the disintegration of the enemy front line, followed by a rapid advance

into the industrial heartland of Germany.

Eight American divisions supported the French in the initial, and highly successful, Aisne-Marne Offensive, whilst a single division aided the British in their subsequent equally successful attack on the Amiens salient. The third and final offensive was carried out almost exclusively by United States Forces. On 12 September some 550,000 troops aided by 260 tanks under the command of Lieutenant Colonel George Patton attacked the St. Mihiel salient, driving the enemy back after four days of bitter fighting. Thereafter the Americans moved north, keeping the Meuse to their right and the Argonne Forest to their left in an attempt to secure the rail junction at Mézières and cut off the German retreat.

In the space of one week General Pershing's staff, inspired by the brilliant Colonel George Marshall, contrived to move 600,000 men, their supplies and equipment from St Mihiel to Verdun to enable the northern thrust to jump off on time, a feat which would have been considered impossible less than ten years earlier.

During the subsequent battle for the Argonne Forest, which lasted for 47 days of often savage hand to hand fighting, the American Army deployed over 1,250,000 men, a force far larger than ever deployed by the United States before.

By 5 November the Americans had crossed the Meuse and were striking west. By now Germany, exhausted, its monarchy in disarray and the Government threatened by revolution,was suing for peace and at 1100 hours on 11 November 1918 the Armistice came into effect.

Although United States losses were minimal compared with those of the European powers (Britain had lost 947,000 men, France 1,400,000, Russia 1,700,000 and Germany 1,800,000 compared with America's 50,280 dead and 200,000 wounded), her contribution to the final victory had been considerable.

The United States had now fought a major war abroad and on equal terms with the great European powers. Her position in the center stage of world policy making was now assured.

Above: American machine-gunners on duty in a French cemetery. The weapon is a French Hotchkiss 8mm machine-gun.

Opposite above: An American infantryman involved in bitter street fighting at Chateau Thierry in May 1918. The Americans were totally inexperienced, but fought well and halted the German advance before themselves going onto the offensive.

Opposite below: Black American troops of the 369th Infantry, 93rd Division. The Army was still segregated with the exception that white officers were mainly in command.

Left: American pilots mainly flew European combat aircraft during the war, and especially French Spads. The Spad VII (above) was a strong, stable fighter: it was replaced in 1917 by the Spad XIII (below) which had a maximum speed of 134 mph.

THE YEARS OF PEACE

Despite fervent pleas from the regular army to retain a standing force of 600,000 men, such was the post-war desire to return to normality that within a year of the Armistice over 3 million men had been demobilized, conscription had been abandoned and the Army reduced to a peacetime strength of only 19,000 officers and 205,000 men.

RUSSIAN INCURSION

Anti-communist sentiments did however overcome the mounting desire for isolationism in the short term. Revolution had broken out in Russia and threatened to envelop the Western democracies. Determined to destroy this menace in its infancy, the United States ordered 5,000 troops to Murmansk to join a British-led expedition against the Northern Red Armies. A further force

of 5,000 was subsequently ordered to the Far East where it remained until April 1920. The Red Armies, under Trotsky's brilliant leadership, proved more of a challenge than expected, whilst service in Russia became increasingly unpopular particularly among Great War veterans awaiting demobilization. Eventually both forces were withdrawn having gained nothing save the distrust and hatred of the new Soviet regime.

THE PERIOD OF REORGANIZATION

After careful study, the National Defense Act of 1920 was passed by Congress in an attempt to create a balanced land force capable of rapid growth in the event of hostilities. A regular army of 17,000 officers and 280,000 men was to be supported by a National Guard of 436,000 and an unquantified officer and enlisted reserve force.

Fact however was not as accommodating as theory. Due to financial restraints the regular army rarely rose above 12,000 officers and 125,000 men until the danger of conflict in the 1930s forced its growth. The Guard averaged no more than 180,000, whilst the non-commissioned reserve proved highly unpopular. Only among the officer reserves, drawn mainly from the ROTC, were allocations actually fulfilled.

Staff reorganization was however more positive. When in 1921 Pershing was promoted to Chief of Staff, an appointment which he had greatly distrusted when serving in the trenches, he began at once to strengthen his position. Three new major branches, the Air Service, the Chemical Warfare Service and the Finance

Department, were created to serve alongside the Infantry and Artillery. The General Staff was reorganized into five divisions; personnel, intelligence, training and operations, supply and war plans. Training continued in the 31 special branch schools whilst the General Staff and Service College at Fort Leavenworth was streamlined and renamed the General Staff School, a

one of the most advanced light bombers in the world whilst the prototype Boeing B-17, or "Flying Fortress," which entered service two years later, was arguably the finest heavy bomber of the decade.

By the time that it went to war the Air Force would boast such aircraft as the Curtiss P-40 Tomahawk and Lockheed P-38 Lightning.

The Army's development of armored fighting vehicles during the same years was, however, less successful. By 1920 the Tank Corps of 5,000 vehicles and 20,000 men had all but disappeared. Although steps were taken to mechanize the ground forces in the 1930s, the necessity for the tank as an independent strike force was simply not appreciated. America lagged far behind Europe in the production and exploitation of the tank and would continue to produce models far inferior to the German Panthers and Tigers throughout the War.

The Infantry, however, fared better. The Springfield was replaced in 1936 by the vastly superior .30-caliber gas-operated semi-automatic Garand M1, whilst the Browning Automatic Rifle, the heavy and unwieldy section support weapon, was supplemented by the .45-caliber Thompson sub-machine-gun, made famous by the Chicago mobsters of the 1920s.

At about the same time the Army introduced the 81mm M1 and 60mm M2 mortars into the infantry, and the 57mm anti-tank gun, the 105mm M3 howitzer and the massive 155mm Long Tom into the artillery, weapons destined to remain in the American arsenal for the next twenty years.

title more appropriate to its duties.

Strangely the Tank Corps, which had done such sterling work in the last few weeks of the War, was largely ignored, remaining a part of the Infantry.

The creation of the Air Corps was particularly significant, although not without its problems and petty intrigues. Brigadier Mitchell, who along with General Trenchard of the Royal Air Force was an unyielding exponent of an independent air wing, willingly risked the unpopularity of his superiors to establish his point. In 1921 he forced an unwilling Navy to allow his bombers to prove their prowess by sinking the old German battleship "Ostfriesland" in Virginia Bay. The ship was sunk and Mitchell claimed an unqualified success, although others were not slow in pointing out that the ship had been unmanned and at anchor at the time of the "attack."

Unwilling to suffer the troublesome Mitchell further, Pershing appointed the more diplomatic Major General Patrick head of the Air Service. Patrick shared Mitchell's faith in the Air Force, but unlike his uncompromising colleague was willing to see it subordinated to overall ground command. Mitchell objected publicly, was court-martialled for insubordination and resigned his commission.

Even without Mitchell's aid the Air Force made steady technical progress. The Martin B-10 twin-engine monoplane introduced in 1934 was

Brigadier Billy Mitchell (center) strongly advocated airpower and was finally court martialled for insubordination.

vious night airborne troops, taking part in Operation Neptune, landed to secure key areas behind the beaches. The British 6th Airborne Division landing in the East secured the Caen Canal and Orne River bridges, the American 82nd Division under General Ridgeway landed near Sainte-Mère-Eglise at the base of the Cotentin Peninsula whilst the 101st Airborne Division under General Maxwell Taylor landed in support to secure the western flank of the invasion area. After extensive air and naval bombardment at 0630 hours, 176,000 soldiers began to come ashore in 4,000 landing craft. Forced by Hitler to keep two armored divisions in reserve, von Rundstedt, in command of the defenses, was unable to react quickly.

Conditions on the five beachheads varied greatly. The US VII Corps under General Lawton landed with comparative ease on Utah Beach in the extreme west due in no small part to the stalwart efforts of the paratroopers dropped in the rear area the night before. In contrast Omaha Beach was a bloodbath. The US V Corps under General Gerow encountered well dug-in artillery and machine-gun posts with the result that they suffered over 3,000 casualties compared with VII Corps' 197 before securing the beachhead.

The British and Canadians, landing at Gold,

Japanese garrison of 22,000 lay dead.

A landing by the 77th Division was made on the Kerama Islands off Okinawa on 26 March, and on Easter Sunday, 1 April 1945, Okinawa itself was attacked. In 83 days of bitter and bloody fighting the soldiers and Marines lost 7,600 killed and 31,807 wounded. The fanatical Japanese who contested virtually every square inch of the island, and who ultimately committed suicide in large numbers, lost 110,000 men dead.

The United States now had its staging post for the all-out air assaults, which were designed to bring the Japanese civilian population to its knees.

THE FINAL VICTORY

During the summer of 1945, the 1,000 Boeing B-29 Superfortresses of XXI Bomber Command conducted incessant raids against the major Japanese cities. Simultaneously, surface ships and submarines blockaded the outer islands. The War in Europe was over and the full Allied might could now be dedicated to the total destruction of Japan. Rumours of horrific treatment metered

out to prisoners of war by their Japanese captors were proving to be horribly accurate, and an enraged public was demanding vengeance.

All expectations were that the Japanese would defend their homeland fanatically, and that up to 1,500,000 Allied casualties might be anticipated. Plans were made for the invasion of Kyushu, the southernmost mainland island, in November 1945, and for the invasion of the main island of Honshu during the spring of 1946.

All plans for the invasion were however cut short when on 6 August 1945 a XX Air Force B-29 bomber dropped an atomic bomb on Hiroshima.

Two days later the Soviet Union declared war on Japan and on 9 August a second bomb was dropped on Nagasaki. Although Japan still had two million men under arms and 10,500 aircraft operational, (of which half were assigned to kamikaze attacks), the Government had no way of knowing how many more atomic bombs remained at the Allies' disposal.

Japan formally surrendered on 14 August 1945. The bloodiest war in the history of the world, which had claimed some 50 million lives, including those of 235,000 American servicemen, was over.

Opposite top right: General MacArthur ratifies the Japanese surrender aboard the USS *Missouri* on 2 September 1945.

Opposite top left: The second atomic bomb to be used fell on Nagasaki on 9 August 1945.

Opposite bottom left: General Yoshio Tachibana signs the surrender of Iwo Jima aboard the USS *Dunlap* on 3 September 1945.

Left: This scene of devastation is Hiroshima after the dropping of a single atomic bomb.

10: KOREA

THE FALL OF THE IRON CURTAIN

Despite the usual protestations from the Army that its ranks should not be completely denuded with the coming of peace, such was the desire for the return to normality that President Truman realised that it would be political suicide not to release the draftees as soon as possible. By the end of 1945, half of the eight million men under arms had been demobilized. By mid-1946 its numbers had been reduced to two million and within a year of that to 680,000 ground troops and 300,000 airmen. The draft was phased out and the military returned to its traditional all-volunteer status.

Yet the world to which the G.I.s returned was far from that which they had left less than five years earlier. Most of America's allies had been reduced to poverty by the war, made worse in many cases by a period of vicious occupation. The Soviet Union had, however, grown in influence and stature within Eastern Europe. Totally uncaring of his soldiers' feelings and of the financial hardship caused them by keeping them in uniform, Stalin refused to demobilize. America had only her fleet and the threat of the atomic bomb to protect her way of life against her one-time ally and now ideological enemy. Within a few years, a series of spies headed by Klaus Fuchs would ensure that the Soviets, too, enjoyed the secret of atomic power.

While the size of the military was being reduced, its planning and operational ability were being enhanced. Under the terms of the National Security Act of 1947, the Air Force was promoted to equal status with the Army and Navy, and a National Security Council to co-ordinate national security was set up. The position of Secretary of Defense, a post enjoying cabinet rank, was introduced, and area commands established throughout the world. In 1949 the Department of Defense, with the Secretary of Defense at its head, was set up, and has changed little since.

THE COLD WAR

Disputes soon arose between the wartime allies over the fate of Germany and Korea. After Russia's failure to remove the Western powers from Berlin by a blockade of the City in 1948-49, an independent Soviet satellite was set up in East Germany. Slowly but surely one sovereign state after another in Eastern Europe succumbed to Stalin, until eventually the "Iron Curtain" prophesied by Winston Churchill in 1946 became a reality.

A mortar is fired in one of the many skirmishes of the Korean War.

Berlin children watch as an aircraft flies in supplies to beat the Soviet blockade of the city in 1948.

The United States responded with a policy of "containment" under the terms of which friendly countries were offered assistance to combat the threat of Communism. In 1947, Congress voted for $400 million to aid Greece and Turkey, and a year later implemented the Marshall Plan, whereby $16 billion was funneled into Western Europe to facilitate its reconstruction.

In 1948, despite earlier specific agreements to facilitate the country's reunity, Korea was divided permanently along the 38th parallel. In response, the United Nations held free elections in the South and later that year established the Republic of Korea in the South. In 1949 both Russia and the United States withdrew their armies of occupation, and the stage for the first great post-war ideological battle was set.

In 1947 the United States signed the American Treaty of Reciprocal Assistance with 21 of her continental neighbours, and in 1949 became one of the first signatories to the North Atlantic Treaty Alliance.

THE KOREAN WAR
While the Western powers had continued to disarm, the Soviet Union and her massive new ally the Chinese People's Republic, maintained and extended their military strength. In 1950 the Soviet Union had two million men under arms, compared with the United States' 640,000.

The inevitable confrontation between the two superpowers came on 25 June 1950, when thousands of soldiers of the North Korean People's Army swept south across the 38th parallel. The 90,000 lightly armed soldiers comprising the South Korean Army proved no match for the 250,000 Communist invaders supported by Soviet-supplied T34/85 tanks. Within three days Seoul had fallen, and the Northern armies were proceeding steadily south on all fronts.

In the absence of the Soviet Union, the United States condemned the aggression unequivocally, authorizing the use of force to resist it. President Truman ordered General MacArthur, based in Japan with the VIII Army, to use all available means to halt the Communists. However, the single armored division and three infantry divisions comprising the VIII Army were all under-strength and ill-equipped to fight a sustained campaign. Unable to wait for reinforcements, MacArthur committed his troops piecemeal, but was unable to do more than slow the enemy advance. By early August the Americans had sustained 6,000 casualties, and their Korean allies a further 70,000. They had been forced back behind the "Pusan Peninsula" in the extreme

Above: US Army medics lift a wounded soldier off a helicopter to carry him to a MASH (Mobile Army Surgical Hospital) tent for emergency treatment.

Left: A mule helps the Korean war effort. Pack animals proved to be invaluable in the rugged terrain and carried on working when machinery broke down.

Above: Superior American weaponry and training compensated for the overwhelming enemy numbers.

Right: A mortar crew in action.

question whether or not flexible response would offer adequate defense to Europe, or whether it would be used as an excuse not to escalate a conflict if only European interests were under threat. Refusing to subjugate his country's future to an American whim, the xenophobic de Gaulle removed France from NATO.

Whatever the shortcomings of "flexible response", the policy did result in a degree of improvement in the equipment and tactics of the regular army. Mechanized and armored divisions were up-gunned, the role of the two airborne divisions was streamlined, and "air cavalry" units, utilizing a combination of armored helicopters and ground troops, were introduced.

Despite the total failure of the Bay of Pigs operation, organized and funded almost exclusively by the CIA, Kennedy remained committed to counter-insurgency operations, championing the cause of the new elite special forces groups specially trained in sabotage and counter-revolutionary activities.

Kennedy won his greatest victory when he forced a brow-beaten and ill-advised Kruschev to back down over the Cuba crisis. During October and November 1962, the Soviet Union attempted to position a number of intermediate missiles in Cuba. Kennedy immediately responded by blockading Cuba and putting his own nuclear facilities on stand-by. In exchange for a promise by the United States not to invade Cuba, (something she had no intention of doing), the Soviets agreed to withdraw the missiles.

Kennedy and his policy of flexible response had won a remarkable victory. Other aspects of his foreign policy were less inspired.

A reconnaissance photograph of a nearly completed missile site in Cuba, October 1962.

11: FROM VIETNAM TO THE PRESENT DAY

American involvement in Vietnam began in 1950 when limited funds and a few advisers were made available to the French, then trying to re-establish post-war control over Indochina. At the time, Ho Chi Minh, the leader of the Communist Viet Minh with its power base in the North was vying with Bao Dai, the French puppet, for control. Weakened by lack of domestic support, and defeated at Dien Bien Phu, France agreed to talks in 1954. The result was that the country was divided along the 17th parallel. 100,000 communist sympathisers moved north leaving an unknown number of Viet Minh behind to act as power bases for later guerilla units, and 800,000 North Vietnamese moved south.

It was clear from the outset that a lasting peace formula had not been found. Both adversaries built up their armies, aided by 400 American advisers in the case of the South, and awaited events.

Having consolidated his position in the North by a policy of ruthless suppression, Ho Chi Minh activated his supporters (now designated the Viet Cong) in the South, and within a short time was dangerously destabilizing the Southern Government. In response to the thinly veiled presence of North Vietnamese regular troops with the Viet Cong, the United States increased the number and scope of its advisers until by 1960 its troops were actually taking the field with front line South Vietnamese units.

Reacting to the support given freely to Ho Chi Minh by China and the Soviet Union, President Kennedy increased American support dramatically, until by 1962 11,000 military personnel, many of them Green Beret specialists, were operational. Still they were unable to prevent the infiltration of the Viet Cong and NVA (North Vietnamese Army) along the Ho Chi Minh Trail.

After the assassination of the unpopular and corrupt President Diem, a period of near anarchy prevailed in the South, during which the Communists grew considerably in power and influence. President Johnson, Kennedy's successor, found himself on the horns of a dilemma. If he were to send more troops the fighting would inevitably escalate, but if he were to hesitate history, and the electorate, would certainly regard

Vietnam was fought in conditions alien to the GI. No amount of training at home could prepare him for the swamps and jungles in which he would be expected to fight.

Opposite: A section of GIs protect the outer perimeter of a fire base against NVA nsurgents in 1966.

Members of the 151st (Ranger) Infantry Long Range Patrol open fire against the enemy. The Ranger in the foreground is armed with an M-16 rifle.

him as the man who lost the war. Eventually, using an attack on United States warships in the Gulf of Tonkin as an excuse, Johnson sought and was granted "carte-blanche" to pursue the war more vigorously.

In February 1965, Army and Marine combat troops went into direct action against the enemy in the Central Highlands, and for the first time targets in the North were bombed. Still enemy pressure grew unabated. The United States responded with more troops, until by the end of 1965 over 180,000 were operational.

Despite a few notable victories, such as that in the Ia Drang Valley, and the popularity of General Westmoreland's search-and-destroy policy, the enemy was not contained, nor was his will to fight weakened. By February 1968 the United States had 490,000 men committed in support of 640,000 Vietnamese. Between them they had killed 180,000 enemy and captured a further 70,000, but still they could not subdue the remaining 240,000 Communist combatants in the field.

Seemingly willing to accept losses often ten times greater than the Americans, the Communist will to win seemed to grow at the very time that American domestic opinion was turning sharply against the War. Ill-equipped, inadequately trained for a jungle war, and some would say badly led, the young American soldier, with an average age of only 19, never fully came to grips with his environment.

THE TET OFFENSIVE

Reconciled to the fact that the forces under his command had neither the manpower nor the resources to defeat the United States in open battle, yet believing that the vast majority of the population in the South hated the Saigon Government sufficiently to countenance its overthrow, General Giap and his Staff planned a complex series of attacks on a series of key cities and provincial capitals.

Strategic points and municiple buildings were to be stormed and held to prove irrefutably that Saigon did not exercise control beyond its own immediate geographical environment. ARVN soldiers who layed down their arms were to be offered an amnesty, whilst the local civilian population was ,to be encouraged to rise in support. Politically it was felt that the Viet Cong would be more welcome than the NVA, who were therefore limited operationally to their strongholds along the border.

Towards the end of 1967. despite ample evidence to the contrary, US Intelligence officers on the ground did not acccept that a large-scale offensive was imminent. Increased infiltration by the Viet Cong into the major population centers, the growth in the size and number of their training camps outside of such towns, the virtual cessation of defections and the new-found optimism manifested by the majority of recently captured prisoners were all indicative of an offensive but not of its scale. Ironically the US

Waiting for action.

10 Sapper Battalion provided the greatest drama. At 2.45 am a small group of Viet Cong who had earlier stolen a taxi and secreted it in a garage close to the main complex rushed the gateway. Fortunately the Military Police on guard were alert and managed to secure the entrance before radioing for assistance. During the suicidal distraction at the gate, other guerrillas blew a hole in the wall to gain entrance to the compound. However at that moment their commander was killed and the others, now lacking direction, made no attempt to enter the main complex. Within six hours Marine and heliborne reinforcements had arrived and the fighting was over. In reality very little damage was sustained by the Embassy. The Ambassador, Ellsworth Bunker, was quite safe (at the outset of the operation he had been escorted to a place of safety, the wine cellar, by his marine guards) and only five US soldiers were killed. However the first newsflash mistakenly reported that the Embassy had been seized and later reports clearly depicted the bodies of the dead Sappers, their blood-soaked brown uniforms a clear testament to the previous night's fighting. United States public opinion would never again fully accept the credibility of the Saigon Government's claim to be the total master of its own country.

During the course of the night the Viet Cong, supported on occassions by NVA soldiers, continued to attack positions in the Saigon area. Two aircraft were destroyed and 20 damaged in an attack by two reinforced battalions on the airbase at Bien Hoa. The French colonial cemetery, its massive headstones offering ideal if ghoulish protection for the defenders, was taken over by the enemy in battalion strength whilst the main military airfield at Tan Son Nhut was brought under attack, by a full regiment with Sapper support. Twenty-three US personnel were killed and another 85 wounded in the attack for the loss of a staggering 962 enemy killed!

During the next few days troops drawn from five US battalions, supported by those ARVN who were not on leave or who had not deserted, were tasked with clearing the city, in some instances block by block. Not trained in street fighting, a mode of warfare more reminiscent of the Phillipines than Vietnam, and faced with an enemy committed to a fight to the death, many commanders relied expressly on air power to suppress enemy strong-holds to the detriment of the local civilian population; a matter which did not go un-noticed by the press. Nearby guerrilla-occupied towns such as Can Tho and My Tho were devastated by air strikes, as a result of which tens of thousands of civillians were injured or rendered homeless, whilst the town of Ben Tre was levelled to the ground. American protestations that 'we had to destroy to save it" met with little support from a confused and increasingly cynical population at home.

THE BATTLE FOR HUE

Hue, the ancient capital of Vietnam nestling on the banks of the Perfume River, was destined to be attacked by no less than six Viet Cong and four NVA battalions, nearly 75,000 men in all!

The focal point of Hue was the Citadel, a massive defensive bastion some two miles in circumference. Once the residence of the Annamese emperors, its brick walls were sixteen feet high and in places between 60 and 100 feet thick. The initial attack on the Citadel, made by the 4th and 6th NVA regiments, was fragmented and only partially successful, leaving the all-important heli-pad, crucial for the introduction of reinforcements, still under US Army control.

The Communist forces tasked with the capture of the rest of the town were however more successful and by day-break all but a few suburbs had been, in the parlance of the North, "liberated."

There followed an orgy of violence in which an estimated 3,000 "class-enemies" were executed. Professional men including doctors, lawyers, teachers and government officials were summarily shot, bayoneted, clubbed to death or simply buried alive until, sickened by the butchery, the North Vietnamese commander ordered the blood-thirsty Viet Cong to cease.

Initially there was marked reluctance among the authorities to use heavy armament to destroy the city in order to save it. However on February, long after the Tet Offensive had been crushed elsewhere, the Government granted permission for aircraft to attack targets outside the Citadel walls. A week later the order was extended to the Citadel itself.

Eventually 18 battalions, four drawn from the US Army, three from the marines and 11 from the ARVN, recaptured the Citadel and with it the city. Attempts by the Communists to withdraw to the east proved disastrous when the retreating forces were ambushed by elements of the US 1st Cavalry Division positioned specifically to counter such a contingency.

Early on the morning of 24th February peace returned to the shattered streets of Hue. By then the US forces, both Army and Marines, had lost 119 killed and 961 wounded. The ARVN, who had demonstrated a high degree of valor throughout the engagement, had lost 363 killed and 1,242 wounded. An estimated 5,000 Communists had died in the City and a further 3,000 in the adjoining countryside, many of them the victims of the 1st Cavalry Division.

Opposite: A Viet Cong sapper lies dead in the garden of the US Embassy in Saigon. Very little damage was actually sustained at the Embassy, but the credibility of the Saigon Government's claim to total mastery of the country was irreparably damaged.

Below: Soldiers of Company A, 30th Ranger Battalion of the ARVN keep in radio contact as they move against the Viet Cong during the Tet offensive.

THE AFTERMATH

During the Offensive as a whole, the Communists lost 32,00 dead and a further 6,000 captured at the expense of only 4,000 defenders. Justifiably the US Army and the ARVN regarded theirs a victory. However public opinion at home, fed a diet of biased and often uninformed television, inter-preted Tet as a defeat. The loss and suffering amongst the innocent civilians, always a problem in war, was highlighted and found to be unaccept-able. General Westmoreland, due anyway for replacement, was promoted to Chief of Staff and his place taken by General Creighton Abrams. More fundamentally, President Johnson felt it

Opposite: ARVN Rangers guard some Viet Cong infiltrators who were captured during street fighting in Cholon.

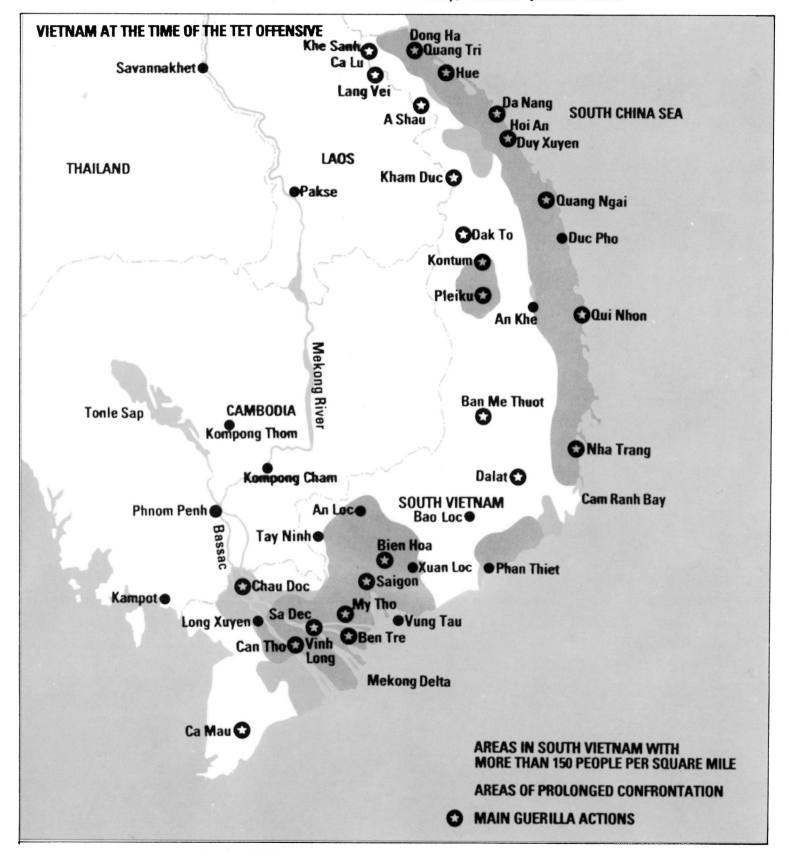

VIETNAM AT THE TIME OF THE TET OFFENSIVE

AREAS IN SOUTH VIETNAM WITH MORE THAN 150 PEOPLE PER SQUARE MILE

AREAS OF PROLONGED CONFRONTATION

MAIN GUERILLA ACTIONS

Main picture: Air Cavalry Regiments were trained to deploy quickly and in force behind enemy lines. Here troop ships land to pick up soldiers after a search and destroy mission near Chu Lai. Support helicopters such as this Chinook (inset left) often acted as 'packhorses'. This one is lifting an M198 155mm howitzer. Helicopters of the Delta force (right inset) wait

politically expedient to halt the bombing of the North and to seek negotiation.

When Nixon replaced Johnson as President a policy of withdrawal in favour of the Vietnamization of the War was actively pursued.

Troop withdrawals in 1969 were accompanied by the first incursions by the Air Force into neutral Cambodia. By now however the War had been lost in the minds of the American civilian public and total evacuation could only be a matter of

time. Although the Communist "Easter Offensive" of 1972 was bloodily rebuffed by the South Vietnamese the United States was by now doing all in its power to distance itself from the fighting. By October 1972 spurred on by a particularly savage spate of bombing of its major cities the North Vietnamese agreed to end the fighting in exchange for an American commitment to withdraw leaving the Vietnamese to settle their differences internally.

on the USS *Nimitz* for the beginning of the ill-fated attempt to rescue the hostages from Iran.

12: THE ARMY TODAY

Immediately upon his assumption of the Presidency in January 1977, President Carter set about the fundamental alteration of the United States' foreign policy. The B-1 bomber program was cancelled, only to be reintroduced at a later date, and naval expenditure was heavily restricted.

Carter's optimistic hope for a more peaceful and secure future was, however, shattered by events. The equanimity of the Middle East was thrown into turmoil in 1979 when the Shah of Iran was deposed by the Ayatollah Khomeini. When subsequently the staff of the embassy in Tehran were seized and held captive by Moslim fundamentalists for 444 days, America was impotent to act, her only attempt at a rescue ending in tragic fiasco. Carter responded by emphasizing the American presence abroad. Suggestions that the army division in South Korea might be withdrawn were quashed, and troops were sent to the Sinai in response to the Camp David Accord, to ensure peace between Israel and Egypt.

Ronald Reagan came to power in 1980 with a promise to "rearm America", and at once set about keeping his word. The Navy was increased, although not to the strength of 600 ships demanded by John Lehman, who subsequently resigned, and a series of inter-continental and medium range missiles were introduced or modernized. Marines were sent to the Lebanon, in many cases tragically to their deaths at the hands of bombers, and in 1982 a multi-service force was despatched to Grenada to thwart Cuban expansionism.

As the Army grew in size and strength so it regained public support. Educational standards increased and the ROTCs were revitalized. The world at present stands poised to see if the two great super-powers can agree to further reductions in their nuclear arsenals. Whether or not they are successful, it is certain that the 781,000 officers, men and women who comprise the regular army, supported by the 700,000 personnel of the National Guard, can be relied upon to support American policy, whether domestic or foreign, wherever and whenever called upon to do so.

A modern combat soldier.

The modern American Army is better equipped than ever before including heavy artillery (main picture) and mobile firepower. The M-1/M Abrams (center left) is now replacing the M-60 (top) as the main battletank while the M-2 Bradley (bottom left and right) and the M-113 APC (center right) now provide the infantry with excellent firepower as well as mobility.

The modern US Army is better armed and equipped than ever before. Figures published by the International insitute of Strategic Studies state that $282.90 bn was voted for defence in 1987 and that over $300.00 bn will be spent throughout 1988. Over 13,300 front line tanks are now operational including 4,500 of the latest M-1/M Abrams.

Today's infantry are transported in over 3,600 Bradely MICVs (Mechanised Infantry Combat Vehicles) and 23,200 APCs including the ubiquitous M-113 many of which are fitted with TOW (Tube Optical Wired) anti-tank weapons.

Increasingly the infantryman himself is being re-equipped with the much improved Colt M-16 A2 rifle. For his personal defence his uniform now includes several life-saving characteristics including the Kevlar "Fritz-hat" helmet so named because of its marked outward similarity to the World War II German headgear.

Since 1987 Special Operations Forces, the cream of the army, have been under the control of the grandiosely named Assistant Secretary of Special Operations and Low Intensity Conflict, a new position within the department of defence. A new special Operations Command, based at Mac-Dill AFB Florida has been set up to incorporate the Rangers, Army Special Forces and special warfare schools into a single integrated fighting concept thus ensuring unanimity of action and purpose in any future emergency.

The US Army in all its facets is stronger, more efficient and better prepared than ever to wage war. It is to be hoped that war will not come again. If however it does, the US Army will certainly give an excellent account of itself.

RANGER, 75th RANGER REGIMENT   **SOLDIER, SPECIAL FORCES GROUP ('GREEN BERETS')**

Above: Fast Action Vehicles (FAV) give the army a high degree of mobility.
Left: A TOW (Tube launched, Optically tracked, Wire command link missile system) is primarily an antitank weapon. It is used to destroy enemy formations of armored vehicles before their firepower can be brought to bear effectively.
Opposite: A team from Signals Corp set up a battlefield communications station.

Overleaf main picture: Members of the 82nd Airborne Division board an Air Force C-141B Starlifter at Port Salines airfield, Grenada. The troops are leaving the island after taking part in Operation Urgent Fury: the invasion of Grenada.
Overleaf inset
82nd Airborne artillery personnel load and fire 105mm howitzers during Operation Urgent Fury.

Index

Page numbers in *italics* refer to illustrations.